TIHANY DESIGN

TIHANY

Adam D. Tihany
with
Nina McCarthy

Introduction by
Paul Goldberger

THE MONACELLI PRESS

DESIGN

First published in the United States of America in 1999 by
The Monacelli Press, Inc.
10 East 92nd Street, New York, New York 10128.

Library of Congress Cataloging-in-Publication Data
Tihany, Adam.
Tihany design / Adam D. Tihany with Nina McCarthy ;
introduction by Paul Goldberger.
p.   cm.
ISBN 1-58093-053-0
1. Tihany, Adam—Themes, motives. 2. Restaurants—Design—
Themes, motives. 3. Architect-designed decorative arts—
Themes, motives. I. McCarthy, Nina. II. Title.
NA737.T494A4   1999
720'.92—dc21   99-30758

Design: Michael Bierut and Esther Bridavsky/Pentagram
Project Consultant: Joseph Publishing Services

Printed and bound in Italy

{ CONTENTS }

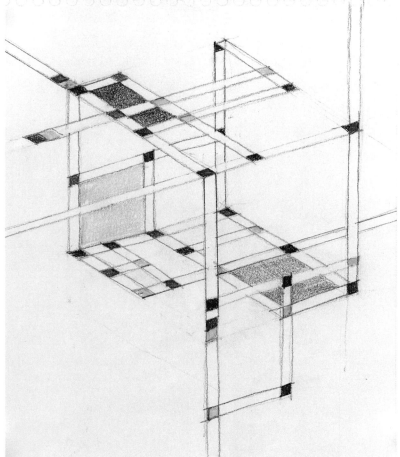

Top: Tihany's 1973
sketch of Mondrian's
Broadway Boogie Woogie
Above: Adam D. Tihany

Preface

One sunny day back in May 1973, at the Museum of Modern Art in New York, I found myself gazing for almost four hours at Piet Mondrian's *Broadway Boogie Woogie*. I had just arrived in the United States.

Back in my hotel room I sketched my interpretation of this masterpiece. For Mondrian, the painting summed up the end of a journey. For me, it was the beginning of one.

And what a journey it has been! From Transylvania (Hungarian language and a Romanian accent) to Jerusalem (Hebrew, spare socialism, the army, the Six Days War) to Milan (Italian food, the student uprising, Umberto Eco as my professor, the emergence of "Italian Style") and finally to New York (fast food, the sexual revolution, California Cuisine, and the birth of my two spectacular children).

It was here in New York that I eventually opened a design atelier. My obsessive need to be involved with the smallest details of every one of my projects induced me to keep my atelier small and productive. I love working with all aspects of design—architecture, interiors, furniture, graphics, and products. But most of all, I enjoy working with the people: the clients who challenge me; my staff who constantly amaze me; and the artists and artisans who influence my work and contribute immensely to all of my projects.

I have been called "on the edge," "cutting the edge," and, at times, "over the edge." However, I would like to think that the most accurate single word to describe my work would be "consistency": consistent harmony between concept, character, and quality.

I am grateful to be a designer and to practice one of the most fascinating and significant professions of the twentieth century. I am awed by the beauty and possibilities of art, literature, poetry, music, theater, and advertising; the joys of watching my children grow, cooking, and cigars; and life with my ever-amazing wife, Marnie. I hope to spend the next fifty years mixing and matching all of the above.

ADAM D. TIHANY

Introduction
Paul Goldberger

It says a great deal about Adam Tihany, surely, that he would reply to a question about the books influencing his work with a copy of Alexander Theroux's *The Secondary Colors,* an extraordinary trio of long essays on the nature, history, and character of orange, purple, and green. It is not a book about design, and its outlook might well be called sensual more than purely visual. *The Secondary Colors* has no pictures, and its real theme is the relationship of culture to these colors—how our culture makes us perceive them, and how they, in turn, make us feel, and how they affect our experience of living.

Theroux's position, balanced tantalizingly between imagination and experience, is at once intellectual and profoundly sensuous, and that is precisely what Adam Tihany aspires to be. He knows that the main focus of his work as a designer, the design of restaurants, is not primarily a cerebral pursuit, nor should it be. He is far too smart, and far too worldly, to indulge in theoretical designs that cannot communicate on the direct, experiential level that restaurant patrons have the right to expect and to demand. He knows that restaurants are entertainment, and theater, and that they succeed best as backdrops for the sensual experience of eating when they provide a sensory appeal of their own.

Yet Tihany knows too that the restaurant that indulges in cheap theater wears quickly, that novelty may provide short-term appeal but not long-term attraction, and that the achievement of the kind of comfort that lasts over time is a complex and subtle process, made all the harder today by the visual sophistication of restaurant-goers. Philip Johnson's job was easier in the 1950s, when the Four Seasons, still the greatest modern restaurant in the United States, was created in the Seagram Building in New York—a high, monumental space in which exquisite paneling, Mies van der Rohe furnishings, and carefully crafted tableware produce a sense of austere grandeur. Since most serious dining up to that point was done in small, plush rooms of no distinction whatsoever, the kinds of places in which red velvet banquettes and white tablecloths symbolized quality, the Four Seasons seemed a new world altogether. Forty years later, the average diner has spent more evenings than he or she can count in modern dining spaces of every stripe, not to mention in restaurants that look like English country houses and Japanese ryokans and Thai cottages and Hollywood warehouses and fifties diners and stadium locker rooms and Victorian haunted houses. It is not so easy at the turn of the twenty-first century for design to make its mark: the restaurant-goer has seen everything.

If "theming" and the prevalence of good modern restaurants in the spirit of the Four Seasons present a kind of double-edged challenge, so does the role of design in the mass marketplace. The Bauhaus dream that good modern design would be available to all was an empty hope fifty years ago, but now it has happened. Places like the Gap, Ikea, Crate & Barrel, and Pottery Barn bring a level of design sophistication to the average community in the United States that did not exist a short while ago. With all of this quality comes homogenization, a sense that things, if better than they once were, are also everywhere the same. This raises the bar still higher for restaurants, which depend, at least to a certain extent, on surprise. People are now accustomed to seeing a certain level of quality everywhere around them, and when it comes to restaurants, they believe themselves to have seen it all. They demand to be both entertained and comforted—to be surprised by the new and cosseted by the familiar, simultaneously.

It is in this environment, demanding and contradictory, that Adam Tihany does his work. His designs are not easily characterized, save to say that they avoid the facile—they are not glib exercises in themes, or period stylistic exercises. If Tihany is not a doctrinaire modernist, he is even less a revivalist. Nothing he has done re-creates historical artifact; indeed, his work tends to steer clear of models of any sort. He is no more inclined to copy the Four Seasons than to duplicate the dining room of the Paris Ritz. Yet it is fair to say that his best work has some of the characteristics of both of these places, and that its real achievement is to bring these worlds into synthesis.

Tihany's work extends around the world, as the somewhat grandiose title of his firm—Adam D. Tihany International, Ltd.—implies, but it is not necessary to look farther than New York to have a sense of the breadth and the ambition of his recent work. A pair of major projects completed in 1997 shows it well: Le Cirque 2000, in the landmark interiors of the Villard Houses on Madison Avenue, part of the New York Palace Hotel, and Jean Georges, in the new Trump International Hotel. The circumstances are similar in one sense—both are elaborate restaurants designed for well-known New York restaurant proprietors in highly visible spaces in major hotels. Yet the problems, and Tihany's solutions, could not be more different.

Le Cirque, designed for Sirio Maccioni, is the updated, relocated version of the restaurant of a legendary proprietor who for years squeezed patrons into a tiny, relatively ordinary dining room on the Upper East Side. Maccioni's unorthodox decision to relocate at the height of his success to a large series of rooms in one of New York's great landmarks, the Villard Houses by McKim, Mead & White, presented Tihany with the challenge of dealing with what were, in effect, two powerful presences—Le Cirque's formidable reputation and the 1882 architecture of McKim, Mead & White. Given the awe in which both were held,

not to mention the New York City Landmarks Preservation Commission's order that the original architecture not be touched, it was logical to assume that Tihany would use this of all moments to attempt an essay in historical correctness. Clean up the elaborate American Renaissance interiors, fill them with flowers and period furniture, and the job, presumably, would be done. And then everyone, after muttering appropriate words of praise, would fall asleep.

Tihany's decision to play off the original architecture, rather than to follow it, seems in retrospect to be less courageous than logical—the only way to force the noble interiors into some kind of dialogue with the modern restaurant within them, and to give the restaurant itself the sense that its move had given it new life. Sirio Maccioni was determined that Le Cirque not be a museum, that it reinvent itself, and Tihany took him at his word, and more. But what is most striking about the design of the new Le Cirque is not the way in which it forces energy into a venerable institution, welcome though that may be, but the way in which it represents an architectural response of enormous sophistication. It is the easiest thing in the world to lie down dead before McKim, Mead & White, and it is a rather fearful thing to challenge them. Tihany engaged McKim (actually, his lesser-known but talented partner, Joseph Wells, who designed the Villard Houses) in a sharp battle of architectural wit, knowing, as far too few preservationists are usually willing to admit, that this architecture is strong enough to take it.

Intense purple velvet chairs, green velvet banquettes, striped fabric panels of red and white and orange and yellow, strong geometries, lamps of Italian colored glass—and, as the climax, a neon hoop across which a clock travels—seem, at first glance, outrageous. Then you realize that Tihany, if born in Transylvania and raised in Israel, is deeply, profoundly, Italian at heart. This is how the Italians always treat their great historic structures, or at least the ones they want to retrofit for contemporary use. They fill them with new things, and they use the new things to force themselves to see the old with new eyes. When we look at the Villard interiors now, they glow behind Tihany's slightly vulgar extravaganza. There was, after all, something a touch vulgar anyway about New York mansions from the Gilded Age; history has tended to sterilize them, to make them more cold and proper, and not the least of Tihany's achievements is to have lit a fire under McKim, Mead & White.

When he turned to a less distinguished building, the Trump International Hotel on Central Park West, where the brilliant chef Jean-Georges Vongerichten was given a major ground-floor space, Tihany might be thought to be able to let himself go even more than at the Villard Houses. After all, here there was almost a blank slate, altogether different from the landmarked Villard interiors. Yet here, too, he responded by going against type, by being not stronger but quieter, by creating a design that is among his most subtle and understated. The building's architecture this time is simple, commercial modernism. Tihany brilliantly understood, as he did at the Villard Houses, how much he could and could not push the underlying architecture—he knew that at Trump, while the building was less special, it was also less tough, less resilient, and that his response to it would have to be quiet, almost gentle.

Tihany took the modernist vocabulary of the building itself and made it softer, much more openly sensual, creating a dining room and café that combine modernist lines with dignity and softness. It is in part an homage to the Four Seasons, but with this less grand space he varied the ceiling plane and the wall planes to create visual interest, adding, among other things, a sculptural composition that resembles a large version of Eileen Gray's famous basketweave screen. Tihany designed everything here, including the checkerboard carpet, the chairs, and the tableware, and the total effect is a glorious oxymoron: minimalism of a shimmering lushness.

Together these two projects demonstrate Tihany's range, and his level of architectural depth. His talents are apparent in numerous other projects as well, from his own Remi in New York, an awkward space rendered grand by a luminous mural and clever use of an exterior arcade to extend the space visually; to the various Bice restaurants, which use light and texture to enrich ordinary rooms; to the Dan Hotels projects in Israel, interiors that gracefully play on the 1950s heritage of Israeli modern design. If Tihany could be deliberately outrageous at Osteria del Circo in Manhattan (designed for Sirio Maccioni's sons) or in Lydia Shire's Pignoli in Boston, both of which seem at times to be less restrained versions of the intense color and emotion of Le Cirque 2000 (and without the magnificence of the Villard Houses as counterpoint), he can also be stunningly restrained and controlled, as in the rooms for the Time Hotel in New York, which are based on the theme of primary colors—an idea Tihany got when reading Alexander Theroux's first book of essays on the psychological and cultural implications of color.

It is not surprising, given Tihany's interest in the design of every aspect of his environments, that he has begun to design and market numerous objects that can stand on their own, such as a line of hardware, including a door handle and a series of hooks, for Valli & Valli; wall lighting for Foscarini; a martini glass and barware for Christofle; sconces for Baldinger; and chairs for several manufacturers, including Pace and McGuire. The objects represent as great a stylistic range as the interiors, and they seem, if anything, to have even greater emotional force than the interiors, as if by compressing his passions into smaller packages Tihany has made them more intense. The martini glass is something of a tour de force, an extravagant glass cone sitting on a glass ball that itself sits atop a silver base from which it detaches when the glass is lifted. If the martini glass has the bravado of Le Cirque, the Baldinger sconces have the understated serenity of Jean Georges: they are exquisite, soft and subtle, with gentle hints of Art Deco. Art Deco is the inspiration for many of Tihany's chair designs for Pace as well, and while the references are occasionally somewhat more literal here, they are never excessively so.

In all of his work—whether it be a complete hotel interior, a restaurant, a chair, or a single dining plate—Tihany's goal is to use design to create a sense of place that is surprising, but not so shocking as to be disquieting; that is memorable, but not so familiar as to be banal; and that is comfortable, but not so easy that it does not offer at least a hint of visual challenge. Tihany is less interested in inventing a new vocabulary than in using existing vocabularies in new ways, and in proving that there is still considerable life to be found in juxtaposing light, color, texture, and symbol. In an age in which so many places look the same, an age in which the notion of the theme park has taken over much of the restaurant business and deeply devalued what authenticity it had, the ability to create some sense of place while still acknowledging all the realities of dining out—the need for physical comfort and visual ease most of all—is a significant achievement in design. "Mood," "feeling," and "atmosphere" are words that are often associated with ordinary places that strive for some degree of visual effect that is beyond their ability to deliver. What makes Adam Tihany's work notable is that he delivers mood, feeling, and atmosphere in spades—and does so in a way that does not offend the serious eye, but excites it.

[A Day in the Life]

This page and overleaf:
Working sessions
in the studio

This page and opposite:
At Remi with partner
Francesco Antonucci
Previous pages: Palladin meeting
with Andrew Young

Above and left: At Freyboy
It's Smoking with
Michael and Robert Frey

Below and bottom: Domus
Sign of the Dove site meeting
with Berge and Joe Santo
Opposite: Aureole
Las Vegas discussions
with Charlie Palmer

Above and opposite:
Dinner with wife Marnie
and Sirio Maccioni at
Le Cirque 2000

"This place is the reason I love designing restaurants,"

is what I told my daughter
Sarah while sitting in the famed
La Coupole in Paris.

{ LA COUPOLE
NEW YORK, NEW YORK
1982 }

Back in 1980, when the owners of the rights to re-create La Coupole in New York approached me to design the space, I initially took the job because of my friendship with them. Little did I know that I would soon become so hooked on restaurant design that it would become a major focus of the next fifteen years of my career.

The creation of La Coupole in New York was a great challenge for many reasons beyond just being my first restaurant design. First, I was dealing with the interpretation of a Parisian institution in a New York home. I wanted to capture the essence and spirit of the original, rather than simply copy it. I had to decide which elements should and could be duplicated, and which required artistic interpretation to fit in with American sensibilities. I also had to create a 1930s patina on a brand new site. The finishes of the original restaurant were prohibitively expensive, so more affordable, creative solutions—such as the broken tile floor as a substitute for the mosaics in the Paris La Coupole—had to be invented in order to maintain some authenticity. One example of the difference between the original restaurant and its American sibling was not only a design decision but also a reflection of the social diversity of the two cultures: while the bar in the Paris restaurant is a secondary element, tucked away in a corner where its patrons are somewhat outcasts from the social scene, in New York the bar is a central feature. There it forms an integral part of the ambience and is a hub of social activity.

Another important issue I had to consider was the sheer size of the restaurant. At the time, there were no cafés in New York that could seat as many as three hundred people. La Coupole would truly be America's first "grand café." We had to wonder whether or not the city could support this kind of establishment. Would we be able to fill so many seats? Finally, when we saw two thousand people lined up in a snowstorm to come to the opening, all of our fears dissolved. La Coupole proceeded to become the hottest spot in New York. Unfortunately, as is often the case in the restaurant business, the management was not prepared to handle the long-term commitment to a major establishment, so La Coupole did not survive. Still, it was a great source of pride for me because it paved the way for other American grand cafés and positioned us at the cutting edge of the restaurant boom of the 1980s.

Above and overleaf:
Dining room
Left: Bar

Sometimes all the elements of a project

fall perfectly into place, as though they were just meant to be.

Such was the case with Tucano and Club A: the client, the chemistry, and the niche in the market were those elements. Not to mention the fact that I was at the ideal age to attempt such an endeavor —experienced enough in design to pull it off, but young enough in spirit to have the energy to get through it! It was, after all, the "big eighties," the heyday of the New York nightclub scene (with Studio 54, Xenon, and Regine's), and all of us young turks were fully immersed.

The owner, Ricardo Amaral, and I hit it off immediately. He was charming, energetic, a creative entrepreneur, and—best of all— Brazilian. He had clubs in South America and was looking for the right angle for one in New York. We traveled to Rio de Janeiro and São Paulo and agreed that what New York really needed was a very chic and sexy European-style nightclub attached to a superb, whimsical restaurant.

In what was a rather bold idea for the time, Ricardo brought Jacques Maximane—then the wunderkind of French cuisine—from Nice to be the chef at Tucano. The design for Tucano was intended to establish the fantasy that would become the guests' entire evening. This was to be a place where the customer could take a mini-vacation—arrive at a tropical paradise for an incredible dinner, then continue into the club to dance the night away in an exquisite environment in which no luxury has been spared.

Until I took on this project, I had not been able to find a place in my career where I could delve into varied facets of design. In America, one was either an interior designer for homes, offices, or hotels; a product designer; an architect; a lighting designer; and so on. There were no comprehensive design ateliers, as in Europe. This was where I realized the opportunities for an all-encompassing range of work in hospitality design. We designed every component for Tucano and Club A: tables, chairs, light fixtures, carpets, fabrics, even ashtrays and accessories. I was able to commission glass artists, sculptors, graphic artists, and carpet mills. No detail was overlooked and all elements were perfectly consistent with each other—a practice I still adhere to today. Tucano and Club A taught me that to custom design each detail shapes the customers' memorable experience. That is the key to the success of an establishment.

Tucano dining room

Above: Club A Bar

Right: Lounge

Above: Club A ladies-
room mural
Opposite: General view

"I like your face. I trust you,"

was all Dino De Laurentiis said when he hired me.

$$\left(\begin{array}{c}\textbf{DDL Foodshow}\\ \text{New York, New York}\\ \text{Beverly Hills, California}\\ 1983\end{array}\right)$$

He didn't know my work, nor did he even want to see anything I had done in the past—from the moment we met, we clicked. We spoke the same language, and I don't just mean Italian. He had a dream of what this project was to be, and I carried it out with a clear vision. Dino's concept of marketing food in theatrical, cinematographic grandeur was novel and appealing to me. Unfortunately, the whole idea was too far ahead of its time. It was going to be years before highly designed gourmet markets would catch on in the United States. We were innovative, larger than life, and exorbitant in quantity and quality —and, most likely, totally intimidating. People poured into the stores, awed by the spectacular displays and design, but the culture for espresso bars and for expensive, gourmet, prepared food did not yet exist. The people simply were not ready.

The concept was to make DDL Foodshow comparable to Peck in Milan, Fauchon in Paris, and Harrod's food court in London. All three DDL Foodshow locations—two in Manhattan and one in Beverly Hills—were massive spaces, laid out so the merchandise would draw people through the space to finally reach the "gastronomia," the rotisserie and prepared-foods section. This was a food spectacle. The lighting,

mostly theatrical spotlights, was specifically created to reinforce the circulation path and lead the customer through all areas. The store included fresh pasta, bread, and pastry sections; America's first walk-up espresso bar where European-style sandwiches were also served; the huge gastronomia area; and in two of the locations, a restaurant. Signature elements that would link all the stores included Mediterranean blue and terra-cotta floor tiles, and brass and wood cabinetry.

DDL Foodshow made a great impression and received abundant press coverage. Unfortunately, as if for one of Dino's movies, the public came only to watch rather than to participate. If this project had opened in 1990, it certainly would have been a runaway success.

This page and opposite:
Food-station details,
Columbus Avenue, New York

This page and opposite:
Details, Beverly Hills, California

*I have always had
a great passion
for Venetian glass.*

[**FOSCARINI**
LIGHTING
1984]

After graduating from the Politecnico di Milano (School of Architecture and Urban Planning in Milan), much of my early professional experience was in the design, development, and production of furniture and furnishings. I was fortunate to have worked with numerous Italian artisans and manufacturers whose knowledge and love for their crafts were inspirational and contagious. From early on, I was captivated by this design process, which could gratify through such clarity of form and purity of materials.

My first encounter with the beauty of Venetian glassmaking came at the furnaces of my friend Luciano Vistosi. While an intern at a design studio in Milan and working on designs for a custom light fixture, I was sent to Murano to learn how glass was made. That trip, the city, its glass, and Luciano would become driving forces in my professional development.

Venice is replete with examples of exquisite antique glass as well as new designs of astounding artistry. This great craft of Venetian glassmaking has evolved over hundreds of years, always simultaneously respecting the past and striving for innovation. Foscarini was the leader in the field of contemporary glass lamps and I was thrilled to be asked to design a line of light fixtures for commercial production. This whimsical collection, Wassily off the Wall, was created as an homage to the great abstract artist Wassily Kandinsky. With my collaborator, Joe Mancini, I developed seven fixtures that three-dimensionally explored one of Kandinsky's favorite theories: the relationship of space and form to color. Foscarini's expertise in glassmaking allowed us to combine a variety of shapes on multilevel planes, with a depth of color unique in commercial fixtures.

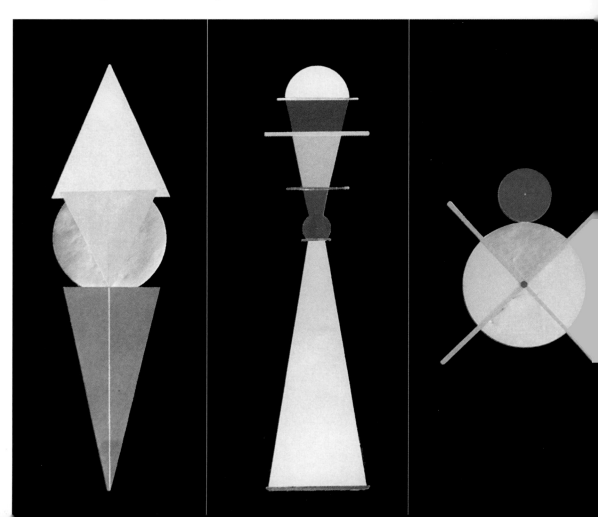

Below: Conceptual
drawings, Wassily off the
Wall light fixtures.

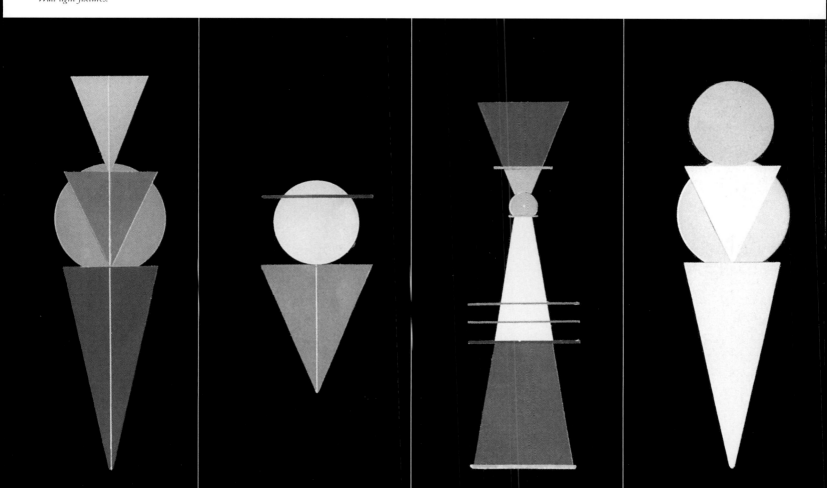

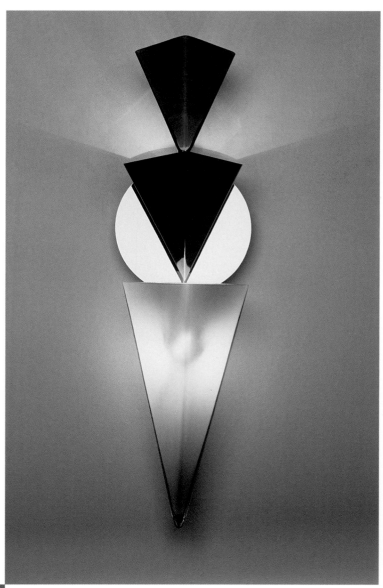

Above: K2 Sconce

Left: K7 Table Lamp

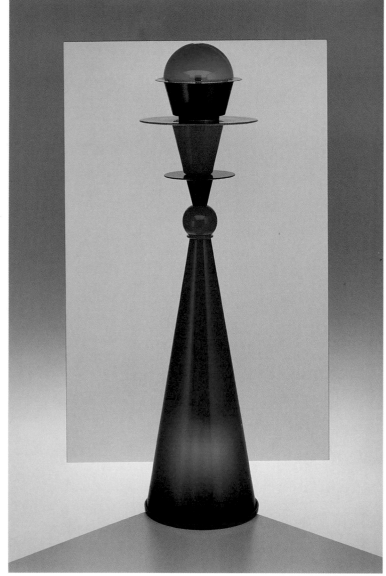

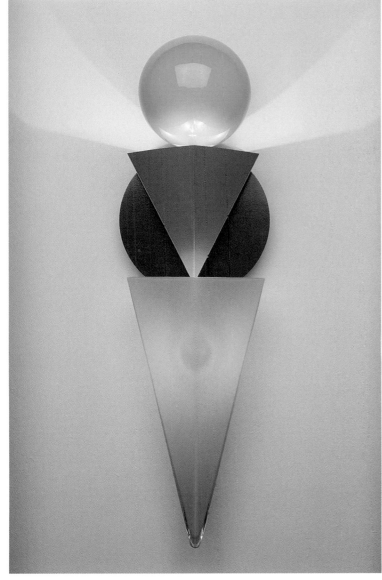

Above: K6 Table Lamp

Left: K3 Sconce

In restaurant design, to

interpret a perception

is more stimulating—and when
done correctly, more valuable—than
simply to cling to authenticity.

{
BICE RESTAURANTS
NEW YORK, NEW YORK
BEVERLY HILLS, CALIFORNIA
PARIS, FRANCE
1987–1991
}

When I was asked by Roberto Ruggieri to re-create the internationally famous Milanese family restaurant Bice in New York, I was intrigued by his desire to find a perfect niche in the New York restaurant environment rather than just to install a copy of this famous institution. New Yorkers then associated modern Italian design with images such as Giorgio Armani fashions and Ferrari automobiles, but their most frequent exposure to Italian restaurant design was the cliché of Italian dining images: tables covered with red-and-white-checkered tablecloths, diners illuminated by a candle that drips down the side of a Chianti bottle. It was time to address the expectations of contemporary restaurant-goers and to create a space that would correspond to their perception of what the modern Italian dining experience was all about.

From the outset, I knew the hope was that Bice New York (1987) would eventually translate to other major cities. This restaurant needed a unique perspective that would stand out anywhere. I realized that Italian Art Deco of the 1920s and 1930s, little used in the United States, would offer a distinctive approach. The style is more of a working-class Deco—less angular and formal than French Art Deco, and not as ornamental and glitzy as American Deco. This inspiration was a starting point from which emerged—with the addition of carefully selected color schemes, fabrics, carpets, and wood tints—a contemporary Italian image.

Each subsequent Bice I designed (Beverly Hills, 1988; Chicago, 1988; Paris, 1991; Palm Beach, 1991; Washington, D.C., 1991; Scottsdale, 1992; and San Diego, 1993) had specific characteristics befitting each location but also maintained essential common features, easily identifiable as the "Bice style." Important to each Bice is its fine woodworking, usually of curly sycamore and mahogany; the pyramidal ceiling vault with trusswork detailing; unique carpeting and striped upholstery fabric; custom-designed chairs and barstools; and the custom sconces of brass and translucent glass. From these details, each Bice could be immediately recognized as a sibling of the others, while each also took on a distinct local flavor and personality.

Above and opposite: Bar,
New York
Overleaf: Dining room, New York

Above: Dining room, Paris

Left: Bar, Paris

Below: Lounge, Paris

Overleaf: Dining room,

Beverly Hills

An important cornerstone of my design philosophy is that

**a great restaurant design
is truly a portrait
of the chef or owner.**

[METRO
NEW YORK, NEW YORK
1988]

This principle had its roots in Metro, a distinct turning point in my career. After a very successful tenure at New York's Odeon in TriBeCa, the late chef Patrick Clark was ready to move uptown and create New York's first upscale American bistro, true American cuisine in an elegant setting. Working so closely with Patrick as both chef and owner, I was able to focus on the relationship between food and its surroundings. I studied in depth his cuisine, temperament, and style. For the first time, I deliberately designed the decor and ambience to complement and celebrate that relationship.

The space that Metro took over had been a very clubby, old, and dark paneled steak house. To help illustrate the new maturity in Patrick's cooking, the room was transformed into a comfortable yet formal layout, complete with leather banquettes around the perimeter and freestanding tables in the center of the main dining room. To reflect the lighter, more upbeat American fare, I refinished all of the original woodwork with new light mahogany paneling, and stenciled antique patterns in the ceilings that were intended to look as if they had been discovered during construction. Like Patrick's personality, Metro had taken on an agreeable, hospitable glow.

Metro should be credited with another first: it showcased the first custom chair I would design for a restaurant that would later be sold commercially. The Metro Chair became an icon of the restaurant, while this element of design became a distinguishing characteristic of many of my projects. To this day, whenever possible, each restaurant I create receives its own custom-designed signature piece that will bear that restaurant's name in the marketplace.

Above: Bar

*Above and
opposite:
Dining room*

Hubert's was the Jean Georges of my young

restaurant design career—my early study in the uses of

architecture as design

and of simple yet exquisite materials.

[
HUBERT'S
NEW YORK, NEW YORK
1988
]

Owners Len Allison and the late Karen Hubert Allison had developed a cutting-edge, cross-cultural cuisine: innovative American fare with strong Japanese influences. Hubert's had been evolving over the course of thirteen years, from Brooklyn to downtown Manhattan to, finally, Park Avenue, where the Allisons brought this cooking style to a level that had not existed on the East Coast. The time was finally right to create the appropriate setting for their innovative cuisine.

The layout of the Hubert's space was complicated: four rooms of varying sizes and heights, which I approached as similar pieces of a grand scheme. I decided to reflect the cultural and culinary combination the Allisons had developed with a design that was subtly Japanese, subtly Art Deco. There was a spiritual harmony in the design that stemmed from the repetition of elements in each space, including glowing golden woods, polished brass, and Murano glass. The walls were painted in mottled ocher tones by my friend —and by this time frequent collaborator—artist Paulin Paris. The windows were covered with translucent silks, metal mesh, and sandblasted glass to create a highly stylized rendition of a classic shoji screen, and similar backlit applications spaced along the walls gave a warm glow to the entire restaurant.

Hubert's year-long endeavor was a productive, uplifting experience. In close collaboration with the wonderful Allison team, I was able to bring a heightened sense of design to New York restaurants.

*Detail of millwork
at entrance*

Above: Main dining room

Right: Maître d' station

Below: Lounge

Opposite: Private

dining room

*There is a magic in the energy
of a true European design
atelier, where the creative flow
of ideas is implemented in
many dimensions of design.*

$\left(\begin{array}{c}\text{TROCADERO}\\\text{FURNITURE}\\\text{1988}\end{array}\right)$

It had long been my dream to establish a design atelier that would encompass the many disciplines of design, from interiors to furniture, products, graphics, and beyond. By 1988, ten years after establishing my New York studio, this dream became a reality with the release of my first line of contract furniture for Trocadero.

After manufacturing many of my custom restaurant furnishings, Gabriele Longoni, owner of the Italian furniture manufacturer Colber, approached me with a novel idea. He wanted to create a commercial entity to manufacture and market a new line of contract seating for the European market that had its origins in the United States. Since it was more common at the time for Americans to admire most things European, and not vice versa, this was a gutsy bet. With the creation of this new company, Trocadero, we found that the European market was indeed open to American style. The line began with its roots in my restaurant furniture designs, from which I was able to create a multitude of complementary pieces. Adding tables, armchairs, sofas, and other furnishings, these complete seating groups became popular for hotels, offices, and other public spaces.

Previous page: Man chair
Left: Savannah chair
Above: Bingo tables
Opposite: Boca Raton
chaise lounge

When I met chef Lydia Shire, I knew immediately
that this exuberant redhead would become an exceptional client and friend.

Her enthusiasm
for opening her own
restaurant was
overwhelming
and contagious.

She had no preconceptions of how she wanted the restaurant to look nor did she profess to be a designer. But she did have a strong view of herself as a woman, a chef, and a restaurateur, and she wanted this space to reflect just that. She handed me a stack of photos that she had taken during her extended world travels, which to me illustrated her zest for life, her love of all things pleasing to the senses, and the importance of various international influences on her cuisine. These photos became my inspiration for what would become Biba, and for what I hoped would be a portrait of Lydia and her unique warmth and hospitality.

To many, this seven-thousand-square-foot space overlooking the Boston Commons might seem an impossible site for a restaurant because of its disjointed two-story layout. We turned this into an asset, however, creating a tapas bar on the ground level and reserving the upper level for the main dining room and chief kitchen. Biba is densely embellished to reflect the international influences on its owner's witty sensibility. Most unusual is the dining room's ceiling, a grid of beams and painted "kilims" based on antique Albanian rugs. We translated this detail throughout the restaurant with the real thing—antique kilims covering the banquettes and a few acting as area rugs over the Brazilian maple and cherry floors. Other international accents were added: a wood-burning pizza oven, an Indian tandoori oven, and a glass-front wine room—

all in full view at the top of the Gaudí-esque staircase, with its custom-designed wrought-iron balusters and red lacquered handrail. Especially effective are Lydia Shire's personal photographs of her travels, which are hung throughout the bar. In the end, they complement perfectly the use of glowing colors, rich materials, and unusual attention to detail that we added to the delicious mix.

Above: Bar
Top and right: Logo and graphics
Opposite: Second-floor wine bar
Overleaf: Dining room

Becoming a restaurant owner has been not only one of the most interesting experiences of my life, but also one of the most valuable to my design career. **At one time or another, I believe everyone wants to own a restaurant.** *I was no exception. After years of involvement in restaurant design, I could no longer resist the lure of being a restaurateur. The ideal opportunity presented itself in 1987.*

[
REMI
NEW YORK, NEW YORK
MEXICO CITY, MEXICO
SANTA MONICA, CALIFORNIA
TEL AVIV, ISRAEL
1987–1994
]

REMI

Chef Francesco Antonucci and I had worked together on various restaurant projects, including DDL Foodshow. Much of the brilliant millwork in these restaurants (as in many of my projects) was executed by Capital Cabinets, owned by Gabe Feuerstein. The three of us quickly realized we shared a passion for the magical city of Venice, Francesco's home, and became great friends. It wasn't long before we were planning to open a restaurant together to bring some Venetian magic to New York. The first Remi was a small space on East Seventy-ninth Street in Manhattan. With its success we were sailing. Remi Santa Monica, with partner Jivan Tabibian, and the move of Remi New York to a large midtown space soon followed. In three short years Remi became a critically acclaimed bicoastal restaurant contender. With the addition of franchised properties in Mexico City and Tel Aviv, we were soon international.

The design of Remi had to leave behind all of the Italian clichés to complement Francesco's menu of modern Venetian dishes. By creating a stylized perception of Venice, I was able to develop a design vocabulary that would make each Remi immediately identifiable while still allowing for adaptations to other locations. *Remi* means "gondolier's oars" in Italian, but I wanted to avoid any obvious thematic references. Updated translations of classic Venetian images subtly suggest a cruise aboard a luxury yacht on the Grand Canal. Details featured in each Remi restaurant include a mahogany bar with a large glass-and-wood porthole, colorful

Moretti Venetian glass chandeliers, striped Brazilian cherry and maple floors, mahogany railings trimmed with brass fittings, and custom-designed mahogany chairs with blue-and-white-striped fabric. Each Remi also has elements that allow it its own distinct personality. A prime example is Remi New York's 120-foot fresco, painted by Paulin Paris, which runs the length of the restaurant. In New York the awkward height and length of the space, as well as the concrete jungle feel of the midtown office building, made this colorful, soaring work essential. No such piece was necessary in Remi Santa Monica, with California's bright seaside just outside the windows.

Top: Logo
Above: Dining room, New York
Left: Bar, New York
Opposite: View from bar, New York

One of the greatest rewards of becoming a restaurateur by night was that it added an entirely new dimension to my day job. For the first time, the problems of the operator were also the problems of the designer. I realized that the front of the house is only half the job. If the design does not achieve a harmonious combination between the front and the back of the house, the restaurant will not be a success no matter how beautiful it may be. There are many operational considerations that designers normally are not aware of, everything from proper placement of service stations to make life easier for the servers (and service quicker for patrons) to designing for ease of maintenance. This firsthand knowledge of every detail of Remi's operation has proven invaluable to each of my subsequent restaurant design projects. As Remi has solidified its fine reputation and status among restaurants and restaurateurs, I am fortunate to have been accepted among these professionals as their equal colleague, as well as a designer.

Opposite: Rialto private party room, New York
Above: Remi To Go gourmet shop, New York
Right: Chef's Table private dining room, New York

Above: Dining room,
Mexico City

*Above: Chef's Table private
dining room, Tel Aviv
Left: Entrance, Mexico City
Below: Dining room, Tel Aviv*

Window treatment detail

Carlo Moretti
Venetian glass collection

I know
furniture.

Furniture design has been my trade since my early days in Italy, and continues to be the basis of much of my work. After the success in Europe of my contract furniture for Trocadero, I was approached by the Rosen family, owners of the Pace Collection, to design a line of residential furnishings for their company in the United States. The Pace Collection has always been well known and respected for its quality craftsmanship and originality, and I was happy to participate. Our collaboration continues to be one of my most fruitful ventures to this day.

My first collection for Pace was inspired by one of my favorite stylistic images: the SS *Normandie* luxury cruise ship of the 1930s. My Grand Lounge Collection consisted of club chairs, dining chairs, and tables. The centerpiece of the collection was the dining table in African crotched mahogany and brushed stainless steel. Each piece was expertly crafted of the finest materials with great attention to detail. I am proud that many of these pieces are still some of Pace's bestsellers and have been seen in the homes of some of America's top celebrities.

With the success of the Grand Lounge Collection, the future of our partnership was secure. Since then, I have designed many new lines of home furnishings for Pace, including the Venezia Collection and retail adaptations of the furniture I designed for Monte's and Le Cirque.

Previous page: Marnie chair
Above: Venezia chair
Right: Rendering of Isadora
dining table
Opposite: Venezia love seat

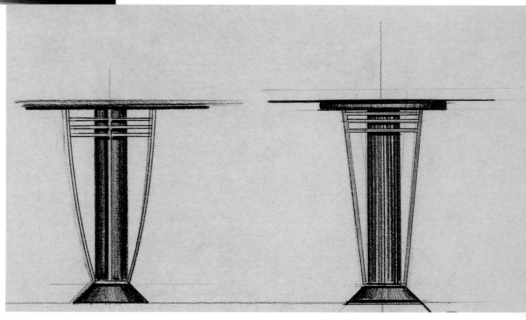

This page and opposite:
Monte's Collection:
dining chair, side table,
disco chair, club chair

Architects
often dream
about the
freedom of
expression
found in
restaurant
design.

I, on the other hand, always dreamed of designing a sexy, sultry bar in Paris.

{ BARETTO
PARIS, FRANCE
1991 }

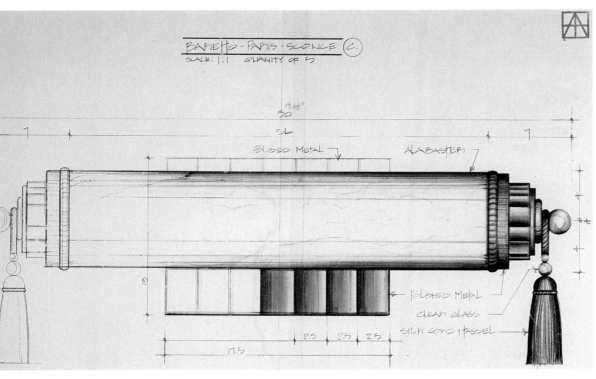

I always had a fascination with Paris of the 1930s . . . stumbling into a small hidden bar where the Bohemian crowd sips a glass of pastis while puffing on Gitanes and discussing poetry, revolution, art, and jazz. Times have changed, but fortunately the imagery prevails. Baretto was my opportunity to interpret that imagery for the 1990s.

Baretto's space and location were ideal for such a bar: intimate enough to be utilized, but not too big to give up its mystique. In the small, exclusive Hôtel de Vigny, Baretto was an alluring discovery that seduced the clientele into another time and place. Classic Art Deco of the 1930s was my inspiration. This period offered a distinct sense of style and opulence, while exhibiting exceptional attention to detail and craftsmanship. I brought artisans from all over the world to create the brilliant work found in every corner of Baretto, including the execution of my custom furnish-

ings, carpets, and light fixtures; the fantasy industrial mural by Paulin Paris; and the magnificent millwork by Efidec. As in the heyday of Art Deco, all of the artisans involved in Baretto shared a common goal: to strive for excellence and innovation in workmanship. The combined efforts of these great talents made this project a unique experience and showed me that superb quality design can be realized when a group of artisans shares a sensibility and understanding of the concept.

Above: Entrance

Left: Lounge

Gundel was a fascinating project from both historical and design perspectives.

The building itself was constructed in 1894 and housed Hungary's premier dining establishment, serving the world's cultural elite until Communism took it over in 1949. At that time, all of the original splendor of Gundel was replaced by formica, plywood, acoustical ceiling tile, and third-rate commercial carpets. As we pulled these materials away, hoping to find a hint of what the original colors, textures, and materials might have been, there was, alas, nothing. Nor were there any photos, drawings, or documentation of the building's original grandeur. The situation was further complicated by the fact that there was no specific design style that could be identified as turn-of-the-century or prewar Budapest, and so I had to develop my own aura of an era. My client, world-renowned restaurateur and consultant George Lang, and his partner, Ronald Lauder, had agreed to go with a more or less Vienna Secession style—very opulent, ornate, and decorative—until, by sheer coincidence at the last minute, we learned of Hungary's general loathing of that look! I could then only create a design from my own perception, rather than the historical reality, of this landmark's former glory.

Twenty thousand of the facility's forty thousand square feet were completely renovated in six months. The main floor space was reworked slightly to add the bar/lounge, situated between the outdoor terrace and main dining areas. On the second floor the ballroom was completely restored and the private living quarters of the original owners were turned into private party, meeting, and prefunction rooms. Finally, the basement was transformed into two wine caves, an homage to the rathskeller tradition.

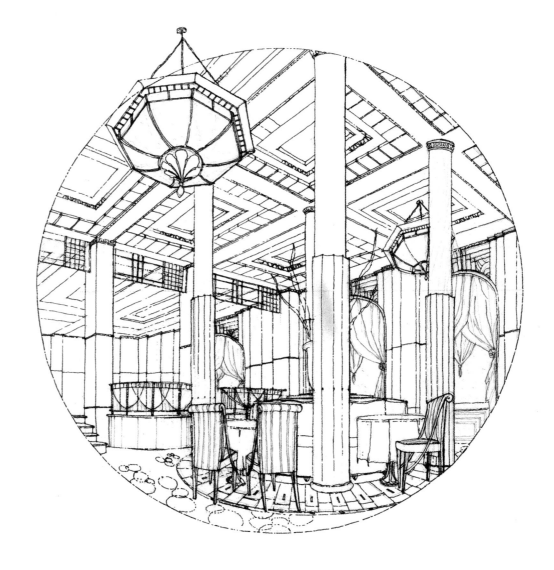

Above: Exterior

Opposite: Rendering
of dining room

Overleaf: Bar

Dubbing the construction site "Operation Desert Storm" because of our six-month schedule for completion, I called upon a list of international resources with whom I had worked in the past. It also didn't hurt that George Lang enlisted the help of Hungary's former minister of public works to orchestrate the construction effort to meet our deadlines. The entire project was an exercise in efficiency. Virtually all of the furnishings were custom designed by me and manufactured in Italy, the millwork and extensive woodwork in the lounge and dining room were executed in Barcelona, fabrics were sent directly from European mills, and local Hungarian artisans provided exceptional ornamental metal- and plasterwork, gilding, and etched glass. Fortunately, despite the accelerated schedule, neither our original design intent nor any of the design details suffered.

In retrospect, Gundel was truly successful in merging design eras and styles. The finished environment is an opulent interior infused by an aura of the glorious first half of the twentieth century, with new elements and treatments that will carry it through the first half of the twenty-first.

Opposite and below:
Main dining room

Top: Bar terrace
Above: Wine cellar tavern
Opposite: Detail of
main dining room

Over the years, I have probably looked at

a thousand china patterns

to help clients decide what would keep the tabletop consistent with their restaurant

design, as well as what would satisfy each chef's culinary presentation.

{ **VILLEROY & BOCH**
CHINA
1992 }

This seemingly simple item can speak volumes about a restaurant's personality and attention to detail. When the prestigious china manufacturer Villeroy & Boch asked me to design my own line of china, it was a task for which I was well prepared.

The first series of plates I created for Villeroy & Boch, Il Mago (Italian for "the magician"), is a set of four show plates. This series is unique in its richness of detail, color, texture—and its sense of humor. According to Villeroy & Boch, Il Mago broke the mold of conventional rim-decorated plate design with its whimsical asymmetrical features and became one of the company's most notable lines of china for restaurants.

Archipiatti, my second china series, took this idea several steps further. Designing a full range of pieces, with serving plates, dinner plates, dessert plates, cups, and saucers, I created Archipiatti specifically to enhance the presentation of any fare. The bold shapes and vibrant colors of this china were chosen so that all of the pieces could work in any combination to make not only the food, but also the whole tabletop, visually stimulating. Villeroy & Boch offers this line of china in both their commercial and retail divisions, a testament to the success of Archipiatti.

When I first asked Wolfgang Puck what he wanted

his Las Vegas Spago to look like, he said simply,

"Design it the way the original one in Los Angeles would

have looked if we had had any budget for it!"

I was happy with the budget, but this was

not Los Angeles. This was

Las Vegas:

America's land of fantasy, glitz, and glitter, on the verge of a new era.

[
SPAGO
LAS VEGAS, NEVADA
1993
]

There was an underlying current of style and sophistication coming to Las Vegas in the early 1990s. Wolf and his wife and partner, Barbara Lazaroff, were at the forefront of this renaissance in the middle of the desert. Some thought they were crazy, but those who know them trusted their foresight. This bet in the biggest gambling town in the world not only paid off but also opened the gates for many of the country's best restaurateurs to follow suit. Las Vegas now has become a boom town for fine dining, in large part due to Wolf and Barbara's pioneering efforts.

Spago Las Vegas is a 16,500-square-foot space that is intended to bring together a multitude of ideas and applications. We had to tackle functional issues such as a mall setting; all-day service; various serving, price, and menu options; and clientele ranging from mid-day noshers to high-rollers and conventioneers on unlimited budgets. Long-held perceptions about the light-filled, high-style Southern California Spago, the celebrity of its owners, and how to make a sophisticated, exuberant atmosphere that would hold its own in Las Vegas without being kitschy presented the others. The result is what has been called by the press a "three-dimensional collage."

Wolf and Barbara's love of color allowed for a vibrant, multicolored palette, while my own desire to fill the space with interesting architectural details led to my creation of an intricate web of angles and depth. From top to bottom, I wanted to offer great visual stimulation: the multicolored fascia of the mezzanine and the staircase risers are done in vibrant glass mosaic tiles; the stair rail is sculpted, burnished steel; and the ceiling is a composition of arched beams and undulating lighting-fixture panels surrounding four tapered twenty-five-foot, copper-clad columns. Finally, James Rosenquist's mural *Time Dust* leads the eye directly to the real attraction of Spago Las Vegas: the open exhibition kitchen that spans the entire back wall of the restaurant.

Ten years ago, who would have thought that Las Vegas would become a fine dining mecca? Wolfgang Puck and Barbara Lazaroff embraced a bold idea, allowed a dramatic design, and brought their sophisticated style to Nevada. Modern pioneers are still finding new ground in the Old West.

*View from café to bar
and maître d' station*

Opposite and below:
Dining-room details
Overleaf: View from mezzanine

Tel Aviv **is one** *of the most* **exciting** *cities* **in the** **world,**

rich in tradition, but hungering for what is new and exciting from around the globe.

International influences come into this Mediterranean town every day, and today's Israelis, being a nation of immigrants, are very receptive to such stimulation. When I was growing up in Jerusalem, the sociopolitical climate was such that enjoying the "good life" was an embarrassment. I had never dined in a restaurant until I was sixteen years old!

Things have changed dramatically over the last ten years. Israelis now believe they deserve to celebrate life and all it has to offer. When I was asked by the Dan Hotels Corporation to design the Dan Panorama Conference Center, it was my chance to contribute to this celebration.

Conference centers in Israel are not only used for corporate functions, conferences, and trade shows but also commonly for weddings, bar and bas mitzvahs, and special family events. I had to walk a fine line between designing a space fanciful enough for a wedding yet serious enough for a shareholders' meeting. With the Dan Panorama I was able to develop a plan that would allow for an extraordinary ballroom that could be divided into many meeting rooms. When the ballroom is open to full capacity it is a spectacle of depth, shape, and color. The intricate details of the coffered ceiling, the circular pattern within the grid of the wall divisions, and the drama of the modern Venetian glass chandeliers by Foscarini are all immediately striking. However, as the room divides into smaller spaces, each division limits the many design details and presents a more subtle, restrained space.

I had the liberty to be a bit more conspicuous with the lobby of the Dan Panorama. This smaller space relates to the design details inside but presents them in a much more concentrated, architectural fashion. The grid and circular patterns translate to the custom carpet, the custom-designed steel-and-glass stair rail, and the bold architecture of the walls and ceiling. This entrance succeeds in two ways: it can add excitement before entering a sedate meeting, as well as act as a subtle prelude to an extravagant gala.

Above: Ballroom at full capacity

Opposite: Conference room

formed by dividing ballroom

Overleaf: Lobby

On a terrace overlooking
Venice's lagoon
one morning, I saw
the
regata storica
("historic regatta"),
a boat race of sleek
movement and
vivid color.

[
REGATA
TEL AVIV, ISRAEL
1996
]

Immediately upon seeing the space for a new café in Tel Aviv, a wall of windows overlooking the bustling waterfront and the shimmering expanse of the Mediterranean, this vision came back to me as a source of inspiration. To bring in the young, casually dressed crowd from the beaches and downtown boulevards, I wanted to convey the spirit of the regatta indoors, as well as offer a fun, easy environment that suited the casual beachfront dining style of this modern city. I also wanted to make a faster, sleeker sister restaurant for my own Remi, located on the floor below, which reflects a more leisurely, luxurious gondola ride in Venice.

To make the transition from outdoors to in, sun and sea are mimicked in a variety of incarnations. Details include undulating ceiling light sculptures that echo the waves of the sea and the bright colors of the sails of other modern regattas. Canvas shades frame the panoramic view of the Mediterranean, custom-designed chairs are nautically striped, and a yellow and blue palette is used throughout. Multicolored terrazzo tabletops offer shimmering hues along the sand-colored marble tiled floor. Finally, with water being such a significant symbol for the restaurant, I added a constantly flowing mosaic pool in the center of the restaurant to bring in the soothing and refreshing sound of the waves lapping the beach.

Regata's atmosphere is whimsical and playful, sophisticated yet unpretentious. It is Israel's answer to the classic European café and reflects the lifestyle of the exciting young clientele who make Tel Aviv come alive.

Above: Logo
Right: Bar

*Above: View
to exhibition kitchen
Right: Pool seating
Overleaf: Dining room*

PIGNOLI
BOSTON, MASSACHUSETTS
1994

With Pignoli, we hoped to create an environment that would transcend boundaries.

Through its name, a combination of *pignoli* ("pine nuts") and *PIGnoli* ("pigtails"), and its blending of nature and fantasy, soft shapes and steel sculpture, we wanted the diner to be completely absorbed by the space and to become part of this fascinating atmosphere.

The first sight upon entering the restaurant is the reception desk, a striking sculpture of steel, wood, and parchment that intertwines soft and hard materials. In the main dining room are custom aluminum and parchment lighting fixtures, zeppelin-like structures seemingly suspended in midair, which aid the perception of immersion into the space. This feeling is carried through along the long back wall of the restaurant, where unusual, free-form brass sculptures appear to transcend the boundary of the space as they emerge from a muted green wall.

The choices for the materials in Pignoli are in keeping with chef Lydia Shire's quest for the finest ingredients and taste sensations. Thus, all the materials are refined and pure: marble and terrazzo, sumptuous primavera and mahogany woods. We intended the interior to enhance the restaurant's sophisticated cuisine without reverting to superfluous thematic diversions or false pretenses. Still, we strove for a consistency of elements, and a little humor. The pigtail and *pignoli* shapes are inescapable on the curled wrought-iron handles of the entry doors, etched-glass partitions, and sculpted bar and reception stations. Even the fanciful terrazzo and marble floor with its inlaid brass, and the chairs we designed for Pignoli—curved green beech wood with slat backs and inlaid pigtails—echo our whimsical curled pigtail.

Lydia and her cuisine have multiple personalities, which we tried to acknowledge when we designed Pignoli. The result is a comfortable, integrated, sophisticated, yet whimsical space.

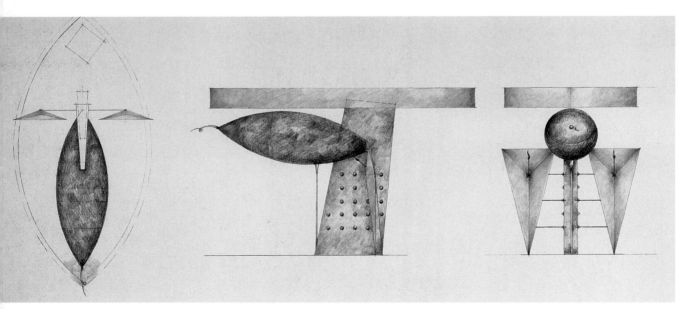

Above: Rendering
of maître d' station
Opposite: Bar
Overleaf: Dining room

$$\left(\begin{array}{c} \textsc{Shun Lee Palace} \\ \textsc{New York, New York} \\ \textsc{1995} \end{array} \right)$$

After twenty years I have learned that any restaurant's main asset is its loyal clientele and esteemed reputation.

A New York landmark of the caliber of Shun Lee Palace deserves quality, luxury, and distinction worthy of its position. Owner Michael Tong decided the time had come to invest in new surroundings to pamper his customers and give them an atmosphere that would reflect their importance to him. For Shun Lee Palace, I created a contemporary East-meets-West version of an ancient emperor's palace—except in this case, the palace gates are open for all to be treated like royalty.

The restaurant unfolds like a complex myth—telling a story with color, materials, and light rather than words. The journey starts in the café at the front of the restaurant, which represents a modern Chinese garden with etched-glass doors that open to the street for outdoor dining.

Overhead is the tail of an etched-glass imperial dragon, which snakes throughout the restaurant. Continuing the story, diners pass through the sculpted cast-bronze gate that leads to a jewel-like chamber. Gem-colored glass mosaics compose the ceiling to make this room regal, inspiring, and intimate.

The final space of the tour is the emperor's inner sanctum, the most lavish main dining room. Walls are covered in deep blue suede, showing off our sconces of copper and steel, which represent ancient shields and swords of royal warriors. Gold-leafed recessed panels display some of Tong's collection of antique Asian artifacts, including ancient snuff boxes and teapots, some from the Ming dynasty. Finally, on the ceiling is the head of the etched imperial dragon, who has wound his way overhead since first trailing his tail through the café.

The blend of Eastern order and Western luxury is a must in a 1990s concept Chinese restaurant. The new Shun Lee Palace conveys the sense of order and serenity that prevails in Asian art and philosophy, but its design also pays homage to the New York style of luxury through the adaptation of traditional colors, symbols, materials, and moods.

Left and opposite:
Main dining room
Overleaf: "Jewel box"
dining room

The charge for Monte's was to create

"the most spectacular private club in London,"

with a mandate for no expenses spared in luxury.

I was asked by my dear friend Andrew Young, the driving force behind the conceptual development of the project, to help fulfill this ambition. At the beginning of the three-year project, many found it hard to imagine that such luxury could be created from a rather inauspicious, four-story structure—pure vintage 1960s architecture. How would we create a club that would rival Annabel's? How would we impart a classic sophistication and an air of exclusivity to such a site? It began with the interior demolition of this ten-thousand-square-foot space and the addition of a two-thousand-square-foot enclosure for a new kitchen. From there, I could work with a clean slate.

To create a seductive atmosphere of luxury and comfortable elegance, I immediately took for my inspiration the grand ocean liners of the 1930s. I created sumptuously elegant interiors using the most opulent materials and paid exceedingly close attention to detail. No nuance was overlooked: the client happily allowed me to design virtually every element of Monte's—the grand staircase, the furnishings on each level, even the restaurant's china. As had been done for those great old ocean liners, I sought to provide something fascinating to see in every room, on every level, at every view.

While each floor has its own composition of furnishings and necessities, an overall cohesiveness prevails so that club members flow easily through Monte's different spaces during the course of the evening—first through the entry and concierge, on to the cocktail lounge and bar, to the restaurant, and finally finishing the evening in the intimate below-ground dance- and nightclub . . . with perhaps a stop at the sumptuous Havana Club cigar shop and lounge. The most striking unifying factor is the grand staircase of nickel and glass, with cobalt glass details, which leads members from story to story. Intricate millwork of rich exotic woods, custom carpeting, glass and bronze detailing and lighting fixtures, rich colorations in all materials and upholstery, and great attention to the ceilings (necessary because of the low ceiling heights on each level) are important features throughout the club, adding a comfort and warm familiarity to each floor.

Monte's could have turned out to be a copy of an old English club, a formal cocoon for a gentrified class. However, by combining the aura of rich tradition with a thoroughly modern attitude, I offered a new outlook on sophistication and elegance for a future generation of private clubs.

Above: Entrance foyer
Opposite top: Havana Club cigar
shop and lounge
Opposite bottom: Rendering
of bar and lounge

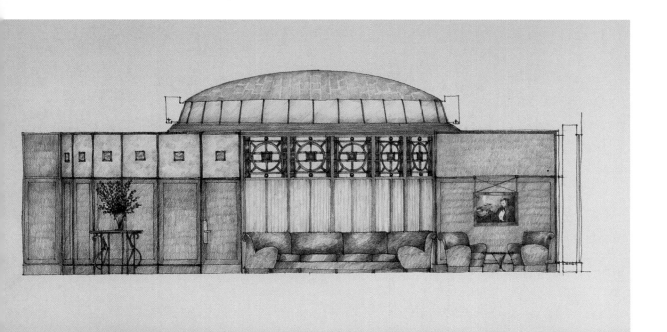

Left: Top-floor bar and lounge

Below: Wine room

Right: Lounge detail

Overleaf: Second-floor restaurant

Opposite and above:
Restaurant details
Overleaf: Below-
ground nightclub

It took five years to design and build the Dan Eilat Resort:

five thrilling,
stimulating,
painstaking,
frustrating,
exhausting,
exciting,
wonderful years.

Above: Entrance to main dining facility

Opposite and overleaf: Main dining facility

Second overleaf, left: Jazz club

Second overleaf, right: Nightclub

Third overleaf: Conference center

*Above: Typical
guest-room bath
Opposite: Typical
guest room*

Above and opposite:
Mega suite
Overleaf: Moby Dick
outdoor dining area

Osteria del Circo was conceived for my good friends, the Maccioni family.
While Sirio Maccioni's famed Le Cirque restaurant was still
in its twenty-year-old incarnation (before we knew we would be creating
his new Le Cirque 2000), Circo was a space for the rest of the family,
with a menu by Sirio's wife, Edigiana, and business managed by their three talented sons,
Mario, Marco, and Mauro. I wanted this restaurant to
reflect the lives of the younger generation—stylish, sexy, hip,
with a bit of familiar humor, yet sophisticated and contemporary Italian.

The family was so well associated with the notion of the circus (in French, *le cirque*) that we decided this was a lucky and appropriate association to continue . . . hence, Circo (Italian for "circus"). Rather than allow this undertaking to become another theme restaurant with Barnum & Bailey memorabilia, I wanted the design to suggest magical memories of a circus through dreamlike details.

The guest at Circo is first welcomed by the *saltimbanco*, a devilish clown etched near the reception desk—he is the true spirit of the restaurant. In the heart of the space, the ceiling soars to what appears to be the remnants of a big top and accommodates some lingering eccentric characters. Mystical, mechanical steel sculptures by J. J. Veronis float silently through the restaurant, each in motion. A story unfolds as a drunken monkey escapes from his partner and threatens to topple an acrobat at center stage; from the canopy above the exhibition kitchen and bakery a ragtag sideshow band of musical clowns performs silently, as if in a dream. With so much action from our figures, I kept the walls bare so that with special lighting effects the walls could continually dance with the shadows of all of our circus acts.

Other motifs throughout this large space make subtle reference to the circus. Using rich materials, colors, and patterns, we were able to present circus rings in the carpet, harlequin patterns on the bar front and etched-glass partitions, and theatrical lighting at the bar and from the "big top."

Despite all there is to see in Circo, I always kept in mind that the star of this show is the food. An exhibition kitchen was created to highlight the cuisine as the restaurant's real performance, and so food enters the tent and takes center ring. All in all, the memory of circus is made even happier, and definitely more delicious. Only minute images of times past are necessary in this rich new world of fantasy culinary amusement for adult children.

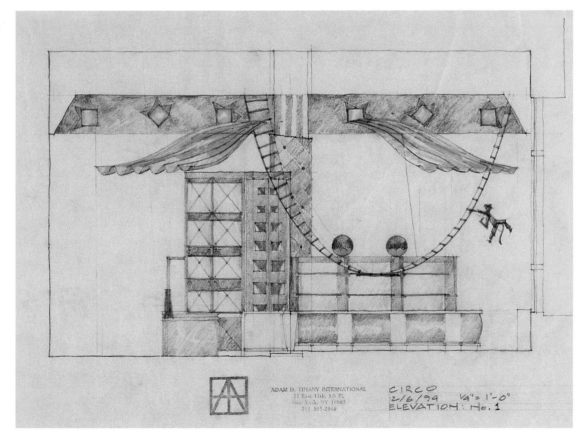

Opposite: Bar

Below: Exhibition kitchen

There are strong philosophical and
design similarities between Circo New York and
Circo Las Vegas, yet there is also a major difference:
while Circo New York evokes memories of a circus past,
Circo Las Vegas steers the imagination toward a

circus of the future.

Left and opposite:
Dining room
Overleaf: Bar and
wine room

I wanted to continue the whimsy
and fun of the original restaurant
while taking this new incarnation
one step further—to create a platform from which Circo can continue to grow and evolve, along
with the Maccionis.

In Circo Las Vegas, I used some of
the original restaurant's signature
elements: J. J. Veronis's kinetic
steel sculptures; harlequin patterns
created from exotic woods; a custom carpet of circus rings; the
suggestion of a tent ceiling in red
and yellow. There are, however,
a few elements that give this
Circo its own unique identity,
particularly the internally lit
bar, the custom circus-ball lighting fixtures, and the state-of-
the-art structural-glass circular
wine room. The striking views
of the water show and lake just
outside Circo's windows—the
restaurant is housed in the famous
Bellagio Hotel—only add to
the circus illusions and culinary
magic inside.

A designer must not only **understand the client,** **but a design must also** *reflect and respect* **its surroundings.**

{ SPAGO
CHICAGO, ILLINOIS
1997 }

The same is true for restaurateurs. Wolfgang Puck and Barbara Lazaroff are very respectful of each of their restaurant's surroundings and attuned to the preferences of the local market. The original Spago in Hollywood and all of its siblings worldwide each have their own definite personality firmly based on the particular community and clientele. With this Spago, I paid homage to Chicago with a grounded, clubby atmosphere and urbane luxury. The little surprises and visual stimulation that Spago is known for are still apparent, but the architectural details are kept more subtle.

To catch the diner's attention at the entrance to the restaurant, I installed a vibrant multicolored terrazzo floor that leads into both the café and the main dining room. A mahogany-and-brass bar separates the space like the prow of a ship, subtly guiding the flow to either side. In the café the warmth of the stucco with inlaid tile at the open grill and the brick pizza oven complement the casual atmosphere. In the main dining room the centerpiece is the open exhibition kitchen surrounded by a dining room of warm colors and rich woods. One of the most intriguing elements of this space is the multidimensional, multihued ceiling. A center sculpture on the ceiling echoes the ship shape at the bar in multicolored beams, so it is as though patrons are looking at the bottom of a Viking ship, oars extending from its base, amber and cobalt glass globes hanging from its center. I have always believed that you express the mood of a restaurant on its ceiling, since it is the only unrestricted surface in the space.

My favorite part of Spago Chicago is the cigar lounge on the second floor—not just the destination but the journey to it. A staircase curves around the elevator column at the entrance to the restaurant; its rail of hand-bent wrought iron directs the customer past the backside of a glass wall that incorporates a see-through fireplace and leads into the cigar bar. It is as though a fireplace in the sky draws the diners upstairs; they move through the space in what is part of the Spago experience.

Wolf and Barbara read astutely what the locals wanted in a fine dining establishment. I believe the design echoes their understanding, offering a comfortable, cosmopolitan atmosphere with no pretense—much like Chicago itself.

Opposite: Elevator core and spiral stair
Below: Second-floor cigar bar and lounge
Overleaf: Dining room with view of exhibition kitchen

$$\left(\begin{array}{c}\text{VILLEROY \& BOCH}\\\text{CIGAR ASHTRAYS}\\1997\end{array}\right)$$

The cigar revolution of the past few years has exposed

my old vice.

"He's a genius!"

"He's out of his mind!"

"How in the world did he come up with something **like this?"**

With Le Cirque 2000 there was no doubt we were performing our own high-wire act while we installed one for Sirio Maccioni in the landmark Villard Houses at the New York Palace Hotel. As I saw it, we had only two choices. One was to go along with the interiors and create a period piece, like Versailles, that would be a beautiful, elegant, and totally intimidating experience.

Choice number two would be to precisely restore the existing architectural features to act as a backdrop to updated, fanciful furnishings. The contemporary elements would give a different vantage point from which to view the original architecture. We were excited by the prospect of creating tension between the two worlds. We took the gamble that they would feed off each other and make each one look better. For us, it worked. For the public, there are those who agree, those who disagree—but either way, everyone has a strong opinion. This was the perfect circus for Sirio.

With the landmark restrictions, we were unable to pierce the walls, floors, or ceilings. Turning this restriction into an asset, our solution was to treat this august space as if a circus had been unpacked inside of it. We installed a back-lit freestanding bar structure that includes three elliptical torchère towers. A clock on a wire travels between the towers and two neon ellipses. All of the furnishings in the restaurant—cocktail tables, club chairs, wing chairs, dining chairs, banquettes, even carpets and china—were designed specifically for the space. No

shape, no color was too bold. In the front dining room we installed etched-glass screens with inset stained-glass circus balls to offset the period murals. High-backed, purple and teal one-armed chairs with clown button details down their backs dance about the room. In the Hunt Room, originally too dark to comfortably serve dinner, we had to create our own new light sources. Striped light towers emanating from the red and yellow leather banquettes were our solution. The brightness of the upholstery and new lighting treatments turned an old, dark-paneled room into a bright, fun space.

Above and opposite:
Gold Room bar
Overleaf: Madison
dining room

Above and opposite:
Madison dining-
room details
Overleaf: Grill Room

NON · EST · IMPERANDVM · CITO · ENIM · EXHAVRIET · ILLOS · NVNOVAM

Le Cirque Las Vegas
presented challenges

completely different from those I faced in New York.

{ **LE CIRQUE**
LAS VEGAS, NEVADA
1998 }

Although there were no landmark issues to address, this time I was designing not only once more for the world's greatest restaurateur/showman, Sirio Maccioni, but also for the world's most discerning hotelier, Steve Wynn. Together they inspired me to create the most lavish, most sophisticated restaurant in Las Vegas without losing any of the Le Cirque spirit.

Images of a seventeenth-century traveling circus came to mind as I began to create Le Cirque Las Vegas. The scene was set with intriguing characters in a decadent, theatrical environment. To re-create this vision, I used only the most luxurious colors and materials: from the alabaster bar to the backlit etched-glass wall panels and the glass-mosaic tile floor, Le Cirque Las Vegas has a jewel-like gleam. The ceiling of multicolored glowing raw silk billows

across the restaurant to ensconce the guests in sumptuous comfort. Faux sharkskin upholstered wall panels complement the striped silks and leathers of the custom banquettes and dining chairs and remind the guest of the pleasures of touch. Completing the scene are Paulin Paris's absorbing, ironic murals, which are framed to create the effect that the guest is safely observing a most unusual circus from a private tent. This is Le Cirque Las Vegas: whimsy and irony viewed from the vantage point of a bygone era's exquisite luxury.

Left and overleaf:
Main dining room
Opposite: Bar

Chef Jean-Georges Vongerichten approached me
to create a restaurant design that would reflect the
significance of his new cuisine and his aspiration
to develop a four-star restaurant while allowing for a
spare, elegant,
yet warm
dining experience.

[
JEAN GEORGES
NEW YORK, NEW YORK
1997
]

The Manhattan space he had selected presented formidable challenges: an unusually shaped space with floor-to-ceiling windows one level up from the Columbus Circle Promenade; the integration to the lobby of the Trump International Hotel and Tower; and the need for availability of food service all day—breakfast, lunch, and dinner—to service the hotel and resident clientele. I gave these issues serious consideration, and with an emphasis on space planning, I arrived at what have proven to be successful solutions.

When developing the concept, I was inspired to design this space much the same way Jean-Georges develops a recipe. I used the geometry of architectural elements and interesting combinations of the finest materials to reflect the bold "architecture" of Jean-Georges's cuisine, which is made from strong, simple ingredients.

To present the architectural theme, the space was designed using a multilevel grid pattern, most obvious in the floor of the café, a stunning hand-laid geometric mosaic of marble and terrazzo, and the varying square-patterned coffered ceilings. Continuing this grid graphic, and offering great visual consistency throughout the space, are three large silver-leafed screens that frame the ample exhibition kitchen; commanding recessed niches for seating in the café and main dining room; the textile patterns used throughout; and the simple, sophisticated china I designed for the restaurant. My fine "ingredients" included the grand zinc bar in the café and the massive shimmering anigre doors that separate the café from the main dining room. This same silvery wood is also used throughout the restaurant in service stations, bar shelving, and the chairs, bar stools, and service trolleys we designed.

By keeping the details subtly well defined and architectural, we were able to give Jean-Georges a clean, sophisticated canvas on which to imprint his spectacular cuisine. Minimal and muted in tone, the design of Jean Georges stands in sharp contrast to some of my more exuberant work. Interestingly, Jean Georges opened at exactly the same time as Le Cirque 2000—and both received four stars from the *New York Times* restaurant critic.

Opposite: Main-dining-room detail
Overleaf: Café

Above: Exhibition kitchen

Opposite: Bar

Upon entering through a door into almost any space, the first item encountered is the door handle. It doesn't get much more basic! Designing a line of door hardware is, by any standard, a designer's dream.

Valli & Valli has been one of the leading hardware manufacturers in the world for decades. Over the years, owner Carlo Valli, long a supporter of good design, has developed a series of product designs by leading architects of our time (including Bellini, Foster, Rossi, Scarpa, and Sottsass). Each has created designs for door knobs, levers, and accessories of unparalleled excellence. I was honored when Carlo asked me to join this roster.

My line of hardware for Valli & Valli includes door levers, pulls and knobs, coat hooks, small hooks, window pulls, and drawer hardware. I am amazed by the amount of technical specification each piece requires and how well Valli & Valli is able to execute these pieces precisely, without losing any of my original design intent. The pieces are distinctly artistic and graceful, yet sleek and contemporary. With my own line from Valli & Valli, I can satisfy my urge to design every detail on a whole new level.

Previous page: Door lever
Below: Small hook
Opposite top left and opposite bottom:
Renderings of drawer pulls
Opposite top right: Large hook

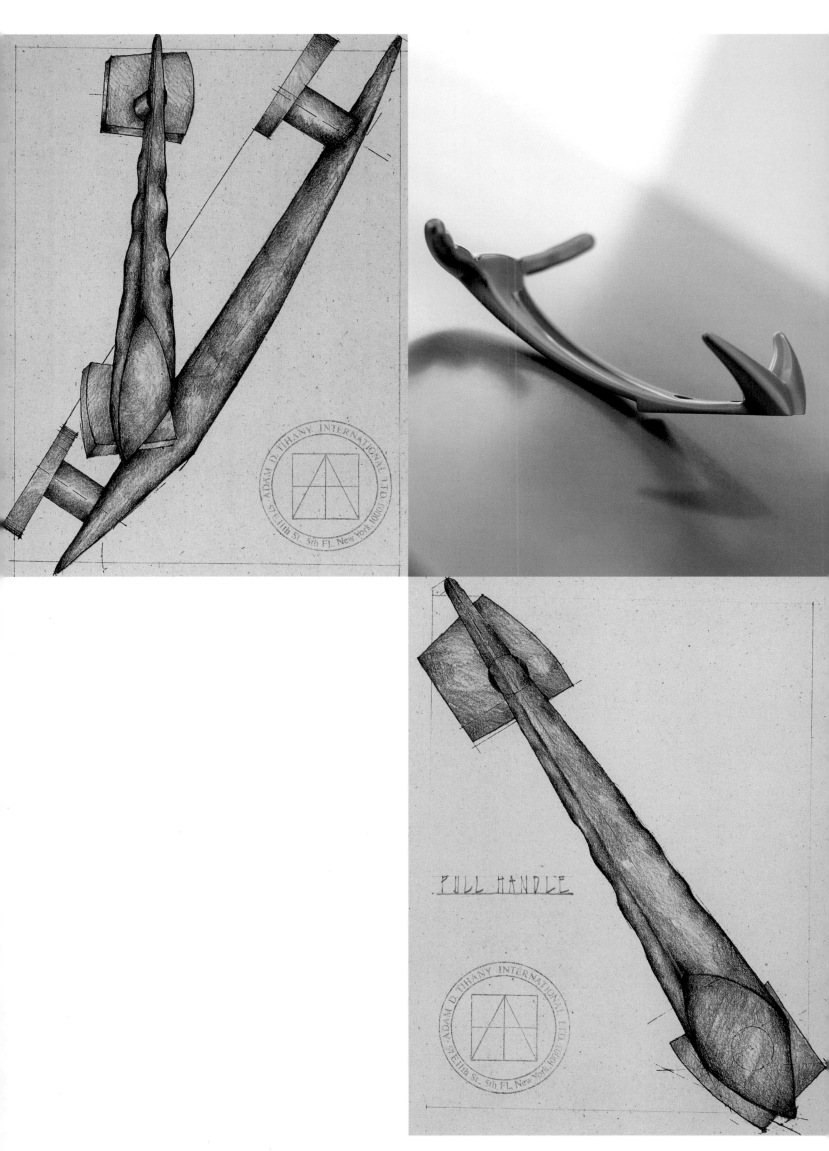

PULL HANDLE

Inagiku at the Waldorf-Astoria

was a project that offered

fascinating intellectual

challenges in addition to the

standard spatial challenges of

designing a restaurant.

This had been one of New York's most prestigious Japanese restaurants for over twenty-two years. With my design, I had to find a balance between giving it an early-twenty-first-century aesthetic and maintaining a level of traditional Japanese decorative components that would make it comfortable for the restaurant's regular, and intensely loyal, clientele.

To conceptualize this fine line, I decided that the most appropriate design solution was to use graphic representations of both traditional and contemporary Japanese elements and present them together in the same space. I wanted to offer a unique perception of these elements both in opposition to, and in harmony with, each other.

Three major design elements best represent this point. First, there is the traditional yin/yang symbol, to which we added a third swirl. Our new yin/yang/yin graphic became a design element, almost a grid pattern, as it was interwoven on the ceilings and etched-glass panels throughout the space. It was also a modern accent on the seemingly vintage Fortuny silk lighting fixtures suspended over the bar. A second element was the use of conventional Japanese wooden slats in less-than-conventional applications. At Inagiku, some of these slats are curved and create an undulating wave pattern for the ceiling in the dining room; others, in warm Australian ash, are in direct contrast to the hard metal pigmented walls by New York artist Nathan Slate Joseph. A final element illustrating the marriage of the traditional and the contemporary offers a bit of whimsy to this strong, elegant space. Playful interpretations of rice grains are everywhere—on custom wall sconces; wall and ceiling sculptures; and most dramatically, as a massive red chandelier over the central bar.

Even the layout of Inagiku illustrates the importance of classic and modern themes. The large conversation-piece bar is most uncommon for a Japanese restaurant, but the smaller nooks of the dining areas are familiar and comforting. There are also the strikingly austere tatami rooms, made culturally orthodox by Japanese architect Hirokazu Kominami, who helped us give our modern treatment an authentic ambience.

All in all, the vast contrasts of Inagiku work together to create a poetic flow. Like a small village, this space offers a choice of environments in which to settle, as well as varied interpretations of thematic Japanese elements of the past and present.

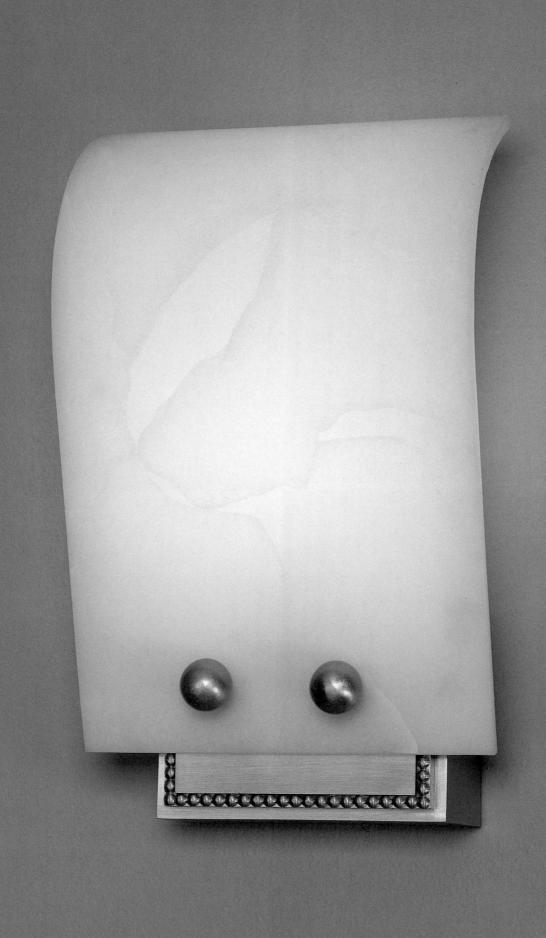

Lighting is of paramount importance for any space,
public or private, but especially so for hospitality projects.
Lighting determines the aura
of the space and creates
the mood, whether
subtle, *exciting,*
sexy, **or bold.**

[
BALDINGER
LIGHTING
1998
]

It can also be too bright, dim, or unflattering, and can make or break an experience. When I was approached by Baldinger Architectural Lighting to design a line of sconces for their designer series, I was intrigued by the idea of applying my experience in creating lighting for large spaces to a series of fixtures.

I had worked with Dan Baldinger and his team on numerous custom fixture designs for a variety of projects and was impressed by the company's knowledge and the quality of their products. They realize the significance of subtlety of detail in lighting fixtures and the delicate balance between new lighting effects and innovative design solutions.

To design this line of sconces, I returned to a favorite and meaningful inspiration: the French Art Deco masters of the 1920s. Each of the three very individual wall fixtures, Ori (meaning "inner light"), Zohar ("aura"), and Bazak ("lightning"), gracefully displays clean lines, fine materials, and attention to detail, and also offers efficient and varied lighting effects.

Previous page: Zohar sconce
Below: Ori sconce
Opposite top left: Rendering
of Bazak sconce
Opposite top right: Bazak sconce
Opposite bottom: Rendering
of Ori sconce

There is only one way to zero in on the personality of a chef: to taste his food.

$$\begin{bmatrix} \textsc{160 Blue} \\ \textsc{Chicago, Illinois} \\ \text{1998} \end{bmatrix}$$

The primary mandate of 160 Blue was to create an upscale contemporary *American bistro that would reflect the attitude of its owner: cutting-edge but never* **trendy, and consistently exuding a quiet elegance.**

Opposite: Dining room
Above left: Bar
Above: Private dining room
Overleaf: Dining room

Possibly the greatest public recognition

I have received for one of my designs is for

a single glass

I created in 1992.

$$\left(\begin{array}{c} \textbf{CHRISTOFLE SILVER} \\ \text{MARTINI GLASS} \\ \text{AND BARWARE COLLECTION} \\ 1998 \end{array}\right)$$

This glass was commissioned by my friend Michel Roux, owner of Carillon Importers, for his well-known Bombay Sapphire Gin ad campaign, and only four prototypes were created. For five years, each time the ad appeared in print, my office turned down multitudes of calls from people asking to purchase my interpretation of the Bombay Sapphire Martini Glass at any price. With some determined cajoling, Michel finally allowed me to acquire the rights to my glass. I was immediately offered an agreement with the famed Christofle silver company of France to produce the glass for the retail market, and within weeks of its release in 1998, the first two hundred limited-edition glasses were completely sold out!

Christofle took great pains to ensure this glass would work for retail consumption, adjusting the size to exact measurement standards and making sure the precarious design would stay stable. Many people are surprised to discover that the silver stand is actually separate from the glass ball, which just rests atop the base. Only the top piece is held when drinking from the glass—almost as if it had been developed for James Bond! In addition to the glass, Christofle commissioned me to design an entire collection of luxury barware to complement the glass. I developed a full line of accessories—including a champagne bucket, wine cooler, cocktail shaker, mixing spoon, and tray—which is now marketed worldwide.

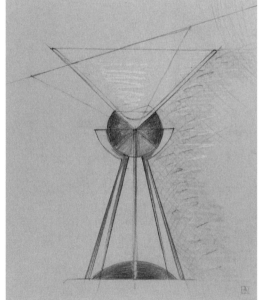

Previous page: Martini glass
Top: Bombay Sapphire Gin ad
Above: Rendering of martini glass
Opposite: Tray, mixing spoon,
champagne bucket, wine cooler

Sometimes it can be difficult to get a client to "think out of the box."

Too often, designers must battle preconceived notions of both the client and the public in order to create something new and different. Robert and Michael Frey, also known as the "Freyboys," were upstarts who successfully broke into the very closed market of cigar retailing. They had a few small cigar shops around the country, but nothing that reflected their personalities or business philosophy. They approached me to create something exceptional, something completely new for the cigar market.

To me, "new" meant avoiding all of the standard cigar clichés: absolutely no leather couches, dark paneling, hunting scenes, or cozy lamplight. Freyboy was to make a sophisticated statement that presented the product image in a bold, hip, and ultra-sleek environment. I approached the task with the use of somewhat unorthodox applications—especially for a cigar shop. For starters, rather than simply keep the square we were given, we pitched the floor plan on a diagonal to accommodate our need for a walk-in humidor, display cases for cigar accessories, and a smoking lounge, as well as to increase the visual frontage of this small, seven-hundred-square-foot space. By creating the angle, passersby could better view the whole shop, an important factor for the high-traffic location in Grand Central Station.

Second, I wanted to use very modern materials and technological effects to accentuate the idea that Freyboy would be *the* cigar shop for the new millennium. Out went the clubby, wood feel and in came the twenty-first century. By placing computer terminals in the cigar lounge, the store offers its clients a place to smoke while still checking on business, a must for busy customers who never want to be out of touch for long. To give the space some movement and additional dimension, I installed a nine-screen video wall that can run anything from cigar images to music videos. Attention to detail, most important in a modern space, is evident throughout the custom cabinetry, display cases, steel-shelved walk-in humidor, and even silver cigar-ashtray door-pulls. One of my favorite elements is the photographic tile floor—like walking on a cloud of smoke—designed for the exclusive use of Freyboy.

Just as cigar smoking has a whole new image thanks to a new, young generation of smokers, the spaces in which they buy and smoke cigars must reflect that new attitude.

Right: Techno lounge
Below: Display detail

Above: Ashtray door-pull detail
Below: View of walk-in humidor
Overleaf: Display
counters and video wall

The renovation of the King David Hotel is, quite simply, the project of a lifetime.

{ THE KING DAVID HOTEL
JERUSALEM, ISRAEL
1998 }

When I was asked by Michael Federmann, owner of the Dan Hotels Corporation, to redesign this most famous hotel in the Middle East, I was overwhelmed with pride and fear. He may as well have asked me to redesign the Wailing Wall!

When I was growing up in Israel, the King David Hotel was a symbol of the best life had to offer. Always filled with world leaders and international celebrities, the King David conveyed a magical aura. To be able to return to my homeland and participate in such history has been a dream come true for a kid from Jerusalem. From the beginning, my hope for the design of the King David was that people would see what I've done and say, "This *is* the King David. This is what I've always imagined it should be."

Walking into the King David Hotel before the renovation, as tired and worn as it was, visitors couldn't help but feel the magic. This majestic old building needed to be brought into the twenty-first century without losing any of its historic character and patina. Although I had extensive experience dealing with public perceptions of iconic images over the course of my career, I never had a project that would expose my work to such public and personal scrutiny. I was amazed to discover how many people felt compelled to give advice on what to do— and what not to do. My mandate was to renovate, update, and modernize every last detail of the hotel without doing anything to change it at all!

For the public spaces I chose to expand on some of the most characteristic elements of the original design and to supplement those with my own interpretations of interiors, furniture, fixtures, and finishes. I worked with a rich, warm palette of golds, beiges, and browns, and added exquisite materials and millwork to reflect the beauty, light, and texture of the golden city of Jerusalem. Some of the old furniture originally designed for the hotel has been remade to be more comfortable and durable, while many of my own furniture designs bring an updated style and sophistication. We created a new bar adjacent to the famous Reading Room; we relocated La Regence restaurant to an unutilized area under the main terrace, gaining a spectacular view of the Old City;

and there is now a two-story balcony space surrounding the front desk and concierge. Every guest room and suite on each of the four floors was gutted, reconfigured, and built anew. Here, the design is completely original and fresh: it is a modern-day incarnation of the beauty and regal character of Jerusalem.

I received quite a bit of praise from the press, the public, and the Dan Hotels Corporation for the redesign of the King David Hotel. But I must admit I felt true success when my mother, Judith, who still lives in Jerusalem, told me how proud she was to tell all her friends that her son was responsible for the new King David Hotel.

Left: Reading Room
Below: Lobby
First overleaf: View
of lobby from entrance
Second overleaf: View to
lobby from bar

Typical deluxe room

*Left: Duplex-suite
bedroom
Below: Duplex-suite
living area*

The first image that comes to my mind when designing a restaurant is a finished space, complete with furniture, fabrics, china, every last detail. At times, the concept includes existing products available in the marketplace. Most of the time, however, the vision features original and new furniture designs.

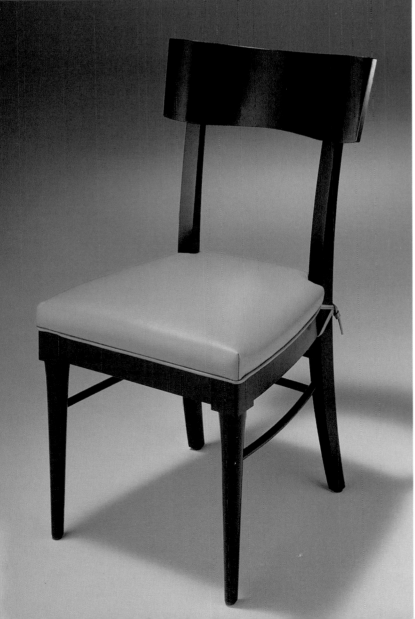

Previous page: Jean Georges dining
Top row: Pignoli front, Pignoli back,
Spago Woven Back, Jean Georges café
Bottom row: Metro, Regata,
160 Blue ribbon back

The chair is of vital importance in a restaurant. With so many in plain view, the chair is one of the strongest visual statements and is the one object that gets used more than any other. I have often found it most natural and time efficient to sketch a silhouette of a new chair rather than search for the suitable fit in a catalog. Commissioning a custom-designed chair can be a daunting proposition for a restaurateur, but by keeping control of the production rights to my designs, I am able to offer the first edition at a fair market price. It is an offer the restaurateur does not refuse! The chairs I have created (all manufactured by Colber of Milan) have not only become symbols for many of the restaurants but also serve as my own signature in those spaces.

Bouchon presented some very interesting
challenges. After years of designing architectural
portraits of chefs and restaurateurs; developing new
and innovative design techniques; and creating
exciting, contemporary perceptions of clichéd icons,

I was asked to design an authentic, yet unique, French bistro.

$$\left(\begin{array}{c} \text{BOUCHON} \\ \text{YOUNTVILLE, CALIFORNIA} \\ \text{1998} \end{array} \right)$$

It had been a long journey since I first did this with La Coupole in 1982, and I was interested to see if I had really learned anything along the way. It was also, quite simply, a fun project commissioned by Thomas Keller, one of America's top chefs, and his brother, Joseph Keller. Their enthusiasm for creating a "new" French bistro in the heart of California's wine country was impossible to resist.

Bouchon is the term used to describe a bistro in the Lyonnais province of France. Like its namesake, this restaurant would be open for breakfast, lunch, and dinner, serving informal French fare. By designing both the interior and exterior of Bouchon, I was able to create a consistent image that could transform with the countryside from morning to night. To attain the authenticity Thomas required, I identified some of the important elements that had to be imported: antique chandeliers, sconces, sideboards, and tables. However, it was important to remember that "authentic" did not have to mean antiquated.

Some elements had to be recreated to give the restaurant contemporary comfort and style. I designed the grand zinc bar, which was magnificently handcrafted in France, as well as my new version of cane bistro chairs, manufactured by the McGuire Furniture Company of San Francisco. The floor is covered with unique concrete tiles that create a bold mosaic in vibrant colors. The space is punctuated by an expansive mural by Paulin Paris of simple yet strong graphic elements that look like a series of individual paintings. With Bouchon, I was able to create a familiar bistro environment without the stereotypical cliché.

Above: View of bar
from dining room
Opposite: Seating area at bar
Overleaf: Dining-room mural

After much market research, the McGuire Furniture Company of San Francisco decided to create their first hospitality-specific collection of chairs. Christopher Berg, president of McGuire, determined that casual yet sophisticated dining was a strong growth segment and embarked on a search for a suitable designer for the new product.

Well-acquainted with McGuire's reputation for superb quality and design, I was thrilled when the company asked me to design this important line. Our intent was to create a new paradigm in the market by pairing stylish design and quality with exceptional comfort, function, and flexibility. The result is the Grand Café Collection.

While each chair and barstool in the Grand Café Collection offers its own unique form, ranging from clean and architectural to graceful and organic, all are characterized by comfort and a depth of design detail. Each piece— Bouchon, Piazza, Galleria, Boulevard, Avenue, and Marché— relies on a unique ensemble of lines, curves, and connections that tests the limits of the materials. Distinctive modifications are the hallmark of this collection, such as Bouchon's seat back, which is a composition of horizontal curves, and its "magazine rack"—a shelf below the seat that adds support to the legs. McGuire's quality of materials and workmanship is unsurpassed, and the Grand Café Collection is making a strong visual statement both in restaurants and in the marketplace.

Previous page: Piazza chair
Above: Boulevard chair
Left: Galleria chair
Below: Marché chair

Above: Avenue chair

Right: Bouchon chair

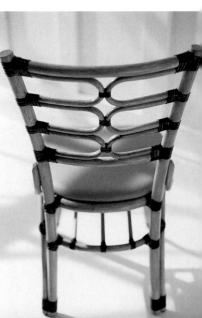

Since I have extensive experience in designing china patterns

for both restaurants and the retail market,

the request from the famed Schönwald porcelain company to design

a new form of china was a fascinating challenge.

Finding a shape that was not only attractive

but also appropriate for the multitude of pieces that would

comprise the line became an in-depth study of dining,

table service, and the age-old art of porcelain making.

$$\left(\quad \begin{array}{c} \text{SCHÖNWALD} \\ \text{PORCELAIN} \\ \text{1999} \end{array} \quad \right)$$

The Premiere Collection consists of a great variety of plate sizes, bowls, serving dishes, cups, saucers, and pitchers (a total of fifty-three pieces). Rather than designing a new geometric shape for the perimeter of the plate, I worked within the standard round shape to find a new depth and dimension. Eventually, I discovered that by raising the inside rim of the plate (between the band and center of plate) we could create an optical illusion, making the entire center of the plate seem to sit higher than its band—the reverse of the typical form. This new shape gives the food a platform on which to stand while offering a clean, sophisticated, and unique look for the table.

Above: Pieces from the
Premiere Collection

There is no greater value to a designer than a client who believes in the designer's **vision.**

[THE TIME HOTEL
NEW YORK, NEW YORK
1999]

Vikram Chatwal, a young New York hotelier, knew he had the right building in the right location to create a unique boutique hotel, and was confident that I was the right person for the job. I identified a rather intellectual concept as the starting point for the design direction, and without hesitation, Vikram was hooked! It was a very modern approach, based on an avant-garde color theory. It was not what the Hampshire Hotels chain was used to and was not an easy sell to the board of directors. Did they want to break out of their niche? Would they be able to compete on such a sophisticated level? Would anyone get it? Eventually Vikram and his father, Sant Chatwal, gave the ultimatum: Tihany's design or nothing. Hence, The Time.

The major challenge in designing The Time was how to take a non-descript hotel and create something fantastic. The only asset the original hotel had going for it was its prime location in New York's hot, thriving Times Square area. To break the mold of the typical boutique hotel (that is, trendy and highbrow), I wanted The Time to deliver intellectual and sensory stimulation while still offering the guest a space that was a calming respite from the city.

The Time's interior scheme, with 36 suites and 164 rooms, is inspired by the selective use of the primary colors: red, blue, and yellow. The guest is presented only one of these three colors in an otherwise neutral room of gray, white, black, and beige. No varying hues, no fades, just true color. The idea is for the guest to see, feel, and even taste a color—to really explore it. Upon entering the red room, for example, the guest will find a red chair, a red bedspread and headboard, a red fruit, and a copy of an essay on red by Alexander Theroux. I wanted to offer people a chance to reflect on color, to understand it, experience it, and learn how it influences their mood.

The public spaces are created in neutral tones as well, with a great bar/lounge on the second floor accessible by a glass elevator from the ground-floor entry hall. The new, stark, ultra-modern front of the first two stories of the building brings the famous Times Square billboard effect to street level. Finally, we created Palladin, famed chef Jean-Louis Palladin's contemporary brasserie, to complement the hotel design and add the necessary culinary cachet to the project.

My intention was to treat each guest as a sensitive and intellectual individual, to provide an opportunity to be stimulated and connected to something as abstract as a color—and perhaps even to learn new sensations along the way. My reward is that the guests actually do "get it."

"The Early Bird"
breakfast valet and
brochure display unit

Above: Suite living area

Opposite: Suite bedroom

Overleaf: Typical room

Biography

Adam D. Tihany was born in Transylvania in 1948 and raised in Jerusalem, Israel. After completing the required three years of service in the Israeli Air Force, he moved to Italy to attend the Politecnico di Milano (School of Architecture and Urban Planning). While at college, Tihany apprenticed in several design studios across Europe, acquiring experience in architecture and product and interior design. He also worked with famed designer Ettore Sottsass on two documentary films about design and architecture in Israel and served as art director for the design magazine *Rassegna Modi Abitari Oggi*.

In 1973, Tihany became an associate at a major Italian design firm. In 1976, he moved to New York to become design director of the firm Unigram. Two years later he established his own design studio and, in 1981, designed his first restaurant, La Coupole. For the past twenty years, hospitality design has been a major focus of Adam D. Tihany International, Ltd. Tihany designs the majority of the furniture and furnishings for his restaurant and hotel projects, and he has licensed many of them, including furniture, light fixtures, china, silver, barware, carpets, and door hardware, to well-known manufacturers.

In 1987, Tihany entered the restaurant business. With his partner, chef Francesco Antonucci, he opened Remi Restaurant in Manhattan and Remi Santa Monica. Franchises in Mexico City and Tel Aviv soon followed. In 1992, Tihany coauthored the cookbook *Venetian Taste*.

Tihany's awards and honors are numerous. He is often featured in media reports about hotels, restaurants, and design, and in 1998 was the subject of CNN's "Pinnacle" program. He is a respected lecturer and judge of design competitions, and he has taught at the School of Visual Arts in New York. In 1991, Tihany was inducted into the Interior Design Hall of Fame, and in 1997, he was recognized in the James Beard Who's Who of the most influential individuals in the restaurant industry.

 for the best support system in the world  **for just being who you are**

for showing me  **the way** for making me believe in  partnerships

 for being a surrogate father  **for the best long-distance relationship ever**

for making Italy  **accessible** for making business and friendship work together

for effortless talent  **and imagination** for showing me the real  Venice

 **for "steeling" the show from time to time**  for an exemplary client-

designer relationship  **for brilliant creativity** for putting up with me

 for making this book happen  for making my work look so good

for getting me everywhere  for missing the photo shoot

The Time Hotel (pages 313–17)
PETER AARON/ESTO, MAMARONECK, NEW YORK

Dan Eilat Resort
RAMI ARNOLD, TEL AVIV, ISRAEL

Baldinger Lighting
COURTESY OF BALDINGER

160 Blue, Le Cirque Las Vegas, Osteria del Circo Las Vegas
MARK BALLOGG, STEINKAMP/BALLOGG,
CHICAGO, ILLINOIS

Bice Paris, Baretto
DONATELLA BRUN, MILAN, ITALY

Remi Mexico City
CLAUDIA COELLO DE RIVERO, MEXICO CITY, MEXICO

Trocadero Furniture, Custom Restaurant Chairs
COURTESY OF COLBER

Freyboy It's Smoking, The Time Hotel (page 310)
GREG DELVES, NEW YORK, NEW YORK

A Day in the Life, Villeroy & Boch Cigar Ashtrays,
Valli & Valli Hardware, Christofle Silver, Schönwald Porcelain
MICHAEL DONNELLY, MIKE DONNELLY PRODUCTIONS,
NEW YORK, NEW YORK

Foscarini Lighting
COURTESY OF FOSCARINI MURANO

Bice New York
KARL FRANCETIC, MIAMI, FLORIDA

Bouchon
MATTHEW HRANEK, NEW YORK, NEW YORK

Remi Tel Aviv, Dan Panorama Conference Center, Regata
MAURIZIO MERCATO, STUDIO WALD, VERONA, ITALY

Metro, Hubert's, Biba, Remi New York, Gundel, Spago Las Vegas,
Pignoli, Shun Lee Palace, Monte's, Osteria del Circo New York,
Spago Chicago, Le Cirque 2000 New York, Jean Georges, Inagiku,
Louis's, The King David Hotel
PETER PAIGE, PETER PAIGE PHOTOGRAPHY,
HARRINGTON PARK, NEW JERSEY

McGuire Chairs
DAVID PETERSON, SAN FRANCISCO, CALIFORNIA

Villeroy & Boch China
PETER PIOPPO, NEW YORK, NEW YORK

La Coupole, Tucano and Club A, DDL Foodshow
MARK ROSS, NEW YORK, NEW YORK

Bice Beverly Hills, Remi Santa Monica
TOSHI YOSHIMI, LOS ANGELES, CALIFORNIA

The Pace Collection
CARL ZAPP, NEW YORK, NEW YORK